Notes on Time

CYNTHIA ERLANDSON

Illustrations by Lacie M. Bollon

authorHOUSE®

AuthorHouse™
1663 Liberty Drive
Bloomington, IN 47403
www.authorhouse.com
Phone: 833-262-8899

Published by AuthorHouse 03/04/2021

ISBN: 978-1-6655-1763-8 (sc)
ISBN: 978-1-6655-1762-1 (e)

Library of Congress Control Number: 2021903558

Print information available on the last page.

Any people depicted in stock imagery provided by Getty Images are models, and such images are being used for illustrative purposes only. Certain stock imagery © Getty Images.

This book is printed on acid-free paper.

Scripture quotations marked NKJV are taken from the New King James Version. Copyright © 1982 by Thomas Nelson, Inc. Used by permission. All rights reserved.

"Words move,
music moves,
only in time...."

— T.S. Eliot, *Four Quartets*

"All art constantly aspires to the condition of music."

— Walter Pater

For all the musicians, composers, and
poets who have inspired me

CONTENTS

Feathered Notes: Time Flies

Open Cadences: Between Times

Key Changes: Transition Times

End Notes: Out of Time

PRELUDE

Bass Notes

> "The tolling bell
> Measures time not our time."
> — T.S. Eliot, *Four Quartets*

Words, music, movement, and time are four elements intrinsically woven into the rhythms of our earthly life, and inextricably interwoven with each other. Words move as they are spoken, as they are sung, as time passes. Words used in elegant forms become musical; elegant music speaks beyond the power of words. Sentences and sonnets, sonatas and symphonies not only move through the seconds, minutes, or hours that we define as time – that we think we can measure and understand – but they can also move us into another sort of time, one that is beyond our intellectual capacity. They can stimulate our desire to catch glimpses, through time, of that mysterious realm we call "eternity."

Words, music, movement, and time weave into our existence various rhythms on which, subconsciously, we learn to rely. One month follows another, and we complain or rejoice – but we notice – when the snow comes too early, or we are given an unexpected "midwinter spring" (another phrase from Eliot's *Four Quartets*). A Christmas carol sung in April or an Easter hymn in October would seem to set the world momentarily askew. And, during those times when our personal worlds do go askew, the celebration of an annual event, or the sound of Westminster chimes ringing four o'clock, the sight and sound of the first robin of spring, or the view and fragrance of a flower that blooms only at this time of year, can reassure us, in our bewilderment, of the invisible but certain pattern beneath all things, like a flowing continuo that moves beneath the complex upper notes of a passacaglia.

The most profound rhythms of a musical or literary masterpiece are reverberations of an even deeper rhythm, which we sense subconsciously as a half-heard presence in our lives, "some earlier music / That men are born remembering." (C.S. Lewis, *"Vowels and Sirens"*) We may think, subconsciously, in something akin to 4/4 time, or iambic pentameter, or perhaps something more exotic – but we are prone to feel uncomfortable when a well-known pattern is disturbed. To avoid becoming overwhelmed with unpredictability, we depend on the flowing rhythms of hours, days, seasons, years, which are the familiar phrases, paragraphs, measures, and movements of life. The clock's ticking, sunrise and sunset, seasonal weather patterns, the turn of the calendar's page, can tend to steady us against sudden jolts, abrupt interruptions, the shocking Surprise Symphony notes in our lives. We rely on those rhythms to assure us that "...even now, in sordid particulars, the eternal design may appear," and that, however sordid those particulars may appear from our point of view, "All things proceed to a joyful consummation." (Eliot, *Murder in the Cathedral*)

On some of our favorite occasions, we say that time "flies." But Time gives the best of itself to us mortals on those rare occasions when it "stands still," when we catch our breath at sudden ineffable insights into the world of eternity. For me, this happens most often when I'm listening to a beautiful piece of music. "This music did not take a long time or a short time. It did not have anything to do with time going by at all." (Carson McCullers, *The Heart is a Lonely Hunter*) It is the vocation of poets, musicians, and other artists to remove the veil (though we can do so only partially) from those rare "timeless moments", to help us to recall the existence of that eternal world which we have been created to desire and to seek, and which is our life's true goal. "Can we not hold the mind and fix it firm so that it may stand still for a moment and for a moment lay hold upon the splendor of eternity which stands forever, and compare it with the times that never stand, and see that it is not comparable?" (St. Augustine, *Confessions*)

— Cynthia Erlandson, Lent 2021

Before Time

"Of vanished knowledge
    Was their intemperate song,
A music that resembled
    Some earlier music
That men are born remembering."

— C.S. Lewis, *Vowels and Sirens*

Orchestra Tuning Up

Is this the way the universe once sounded?
A mass confusion of discordant trumpets,
Flutes, horns, and violins like baffled comets
Without a geometric course, confounded?

Can this be how the universe was founded?
An orchestra of galaxies in commotion,
Celestial bodies bent upon collision,
Spinning around infinity, surrounded

By instrumental and galactic clamor –
Drums, cymbals, bursting stars and unformed planets,
Crashing asteroids and untuned clarinets?
Outside the pit, eternity's conductor,

Unseen, hears all the discord in the cosmos
Of music; steps out from its restless shadows,
Aligns and orchestrates its muddled matter,
Arranging measured sounds in perfect order

And, lifting his baton, already hears
The music of Pythagorean spheres.

Bilingual

Creator of the Note and Word
By which your mystic voice is heard
Within the omnipresent chord
Which says and sings that You are Lord –

You have created Word and Note
To speak what, from the first, you wrote
In sky and earth and human heart:
Your truth in sound and sense and art.

Deep words enhanced in harmony,
Rich symbols swelled in symphony,
And notes that lift a well-tuned phrase
Of poetry, repeat your praise.

May melody intoned in rhyme
Reverberate through space and time;
With rhythmic eloquence, may we
Transcribe your tune's profundity.

Let earthly lyric language pour
Your fame in full-toned metaphor,
Till overtones from heaven ring,
Exalting Word and Music's King.

Seasons' Tempo

"To everything there is a season, a time for every purpose under heaven."

— Ecclesiastes 3:1 (NKJV)

"We do not want merely to see beauty, though, God knows, that is bounty enough. We want something else which can hardly be put into words – to be united with the beauty we see, to pass into it, to receive it into ourselves, to bathe in it, to become part of it."

— C.S. Lewis, The Weight of Glory

In Newlywed Spring

In newlywed spring, when trees are dressed
Like brides and bridesmaids, white and pink,
   Then every guest
   Will down a drink
Of air to drown dull winter's grays.

In jewel-red summer, when roses swarm
Like bees on the hives of their emerald bushes,
   Their perfume, like warm
   New honey, luscious,
Will sunnily run through summer's bright days.

In newly-red autumn, when trees are transforming
Like actresses changing their hair or their dresses,
   They thrill to performing;
   Their drama impresses
The audience, applauding along with the leaves.

When newly dead branches begin to break
And drop like dry bones on the brittle brown leaves,
   And the sky is ice-bleak
   And the mournful wind heaves,
Then again it is winter, and all color grieves.

Dandelions

"… all the days of his vain life, which he passes like a shadow …"

— Ecclesiastes 6: 12 (NKJV)

As I stepped out one morning,
I saw across the lawn
A yellow audience watching
The spreading light of dawn
As last night's black was turning
To purple-pink. The sun
Was not at the horizon
Quite yet; yet, looking down,
I thought it must have risen,
Because the gold, unmown,
New dandelions shocked my eyes
Like many tiny suns.
Or else, an unseen magic wand
Had turned green lawns to blinding blonde
Young heads that all were nodding
In April's festive wind,
As if they were applauding
The colorful surprise
Of daybreak's vibrant skies.

A few sunrises later,
When fiery dawn had faded,
I looked across the crowded
Front lawn. No yellow-hatted
Sky-watchers celebrated
The day. Now, all gray-headed,
They looked much less elated –
And out of the blue, I was stunned
By the stark reflection that dawned

On me (as if these short-lived flowers
Had turned into unwanted mirrors):
I would be gray and old
Some day. I watched their cloud
Which hung above the yard;
It cast a ghostly shroud
Upon an aging world.
And then a taunting gust
Stripped all the flowers bald,
Scattering their hair like so much dust.

Summer Sunrise

In cool earliness of late July
A single ray
Warms the crotch of the adolescent tree.
A luminous serenity
                    suspended
In the orange western sky
                        holds
Its breath in waiting for impending day.
But now the east proves dawn's tranquility
A cool illusion only
When from the sky's split womb
The violence of birth
Brings forth a sun.

Morning Prayer

Oh Lord whose brilliance fills the bursting world,
I thank You for waking me with summer's honeysuckle air
through the window; for kindly making me aware
of quiet percussive leaves, and voices with wings
and for walking with me past lilacs lying dormant till future springs.
All laud to You for the circus of sinewy squirrels athletically springing
from limb to limb while high above them, singing
from thinner, treble-clef branches, cardinals seize
the day, unseen, with their jubilant melodies,
and lilies silently ring deep harmonies
that You hear fully (though I can only hear
in part – being finite – with my inner ear);
and for the choir of robins that join with euphonious flair
this multisensory matins service echoed everywhere,
calling the waking world to morning prayer.

Fireworks and Fireflies

In late sunlit Junes and magnificent early Julys,
Fireworks beat like drumsticks against the sky's
Tight skin of sensational sunsets that last until ten.
Soundlessly, wizards of light, the fireflies,
Flash over the grass like sparklers, dazzle our eyes
With their tiny torches. Fleeting, evanescent,
Festive, they vanish to reappear in a moment
In some other place, materializing again,
A visible tempo of heartbeats, their cool blaze
Energizing electric summer days.

Two Tone Poems at Twilight

Cicada Toccata

The invertebrates' reverberating voices in staccatos
Chant a tempo in prestissimo. Continuous vibratos
In the trilling of their timbals in their trillions from the trees
(Undivided into measures, not melodic or harmonic)
Drone an undertone of stillness while their soundwaves spread like
    heat.
Percussively accompanied by aspen-clapping breeze,
Quickly ticking sixty-fourth notes, soon their forte is symphonic.
While frenetically continuing the unrelenting beat –
Pulsing, almost melismatic – now chromatically they climb,
Still ascending in crescendos, then returning to the tonic
In invisible parabolas of stationary time.

Cricket Cantata

In sunset's fire, the cricket choir (despite
Slight syncopation) chants
Their tranquil summer sequences
Of monotonic Vespers
In restful yet relentless frequencies'
Persistent whispers.
Even evening's half-attentive listener, not quite
Aware of this rhythmic Compline's prayer
Becomes compelled, entranced
By mesmerizing dotted notes that hang in windless air.

Summer Evening Sounds

The cicadas are mowing the air
While a gardener buzzes his lawn
And the crickets continue the prayer
They began at dawn.

The engine of rush-hour hums
With its stereos' gut-bruising noises;
Their thunder of synthesized drums
Effaces our voices.

Bright-vested roadworkers' drills
Make a din as they dig in the street,
While the red-breasted robins' sweet
Notes fill the intervals.

Other songbirds have gone away
To meditate for the night
But the jarring rasp of a jay
Scratches the twilight.

Air conditioners' constant drone
Persists after dark; day's warm breeze
Has gone to sleep with the sun
Behind the trees.

Autumn Ecstasy

In ecstasy has autumn come
With burning bush, chrysanthemum,
And quaking aspens shaking fast
While crackling oak leaves shiver past
The pumpkinned porches bright and brown,
And branches' clothes fall lightly down
From limbs that clap and brave the cold.
The naked branches lose their gold
To raked-up piles of sweet decay,
While clouds' and winds' exuberant play
Joins in the brilliant synergy,
And fiery orange energy
Blows summer's lethargy away.

Between

Gracious God, for this glorious day poured
From your upsidedown goblet the size of the scarlet-rimmed skies,
We raise our praise as a longstemmed glass that glints
With intimations of Your higher world's glow,
Trying to catch the overflow that hints
At things not known by sight – yet partly known
From the million vermilion maple leaves quavering down,
Spilling over the lip of our lifted cup. Squinting
At the warm orange border of the world, where the sun
Is rising like coal-baked bread nearly done,
We brace, full-fed, against the tart burgundy taste,
The fallen yet savory flavor of this Eden-touched place
As You decant your bouquet of autumn favor into our brimming cup,
Your love gushing down, we reaching up.

Rhapsody in Red

Extravagant – lavish – the color of love –
October displays in a gala of grandeur
Its bunches of berries and apples, alive
In scarlet and crimson. With sun-sparkled splendor
The winesaps and fuji shine claret and rose –
Blush garnet and burgundy, ruby and rose –
Extravagant, lavish, the color of love.

Ripe crabapples, warmed by the mid-autumn sun,
Start dropping and rupturing onto the lawn,
Releasing their tartness – a fragrance as dense as
The oven-baked flavor of crisp apple dishes,
Or fine vintage wine that enraptures the palate.
Olfactory flashbacks will double-expose
Remembrance more vivid than berries' wet palette,
Reviving the cravings of more than five senses.
Beyond burnished beauty, surpassing delicious,
This apple- and cherry-bright garland that glows
Gives a lively collection of flavors to render,
In cranberry-crimson, a radiant splendor –
In bracelets of coral, a fruit-jeweled splendor.

Sleek Jonathan apples, profuse like desire,
Strong Japanese maples like juice-tinted fire,
All quiver with living as if their brief fame –
Unfading, unfailing, an infinite flame –
Will flourish forever – will never expire –
Will live on forever, an undying fire,
In lavish, extravagant colors of love.

Portrait of an Early Autumn Morning

"i thank You God for most this amazing day..." — e.e. cummings

thanks be to God for the early pearlized dawn-marbled dome:
for its backlit polychrome smears streaking unsheared flocks
    of cloud clusters still asleep;
for cumulus trees blazing goldleaf in drapes of sheer sunrise that
    gauzily slope
            through their sheaves of translucent, finger-cymbal leaves
                softly shaken by transparent hands of breeze.
and praise for their flapping down in flocks, blurred
    in their unhurried downward spiral, brighter
        than dawnlight on their first and last flight
        through autumn's iridescent air;
for their feathering the ground around our feet,
  and for the leftover summer's heat
    baking decomposing leaves that leave their lingering myrrh:
        a rare invisible incense distilling bittersweet remembrance,
            persistently rising in its intense blessed-are-the-dead sweet scent
                more comforting
                than spring.

October Sunrise

The sunlight and wind, collaborating,
Both in a moment descend, cascading
Down waterfall-willows-turned-yellow that line
A short block of street. Their leaves suddenly shine
With amplified lamplight, crisp fringes vibrating
In rushing percussion: a rhythm in shading,
A musical palette of color and line
Whose bright baroque beauty too soon will be fading.

After the Fall

In late October, when the leaves are down
Around our feet instead of overhead
Where lately they had flaunted orange-red
Bouquets with goldleaf trim – a sunlit crown –
They vaunt their vivid hues, untinged with brown
Foreshadowing. In maple flames unhaunted
By death for these few days, they blaze undaunted
In sub-tree circles everywhere in town.

Theme and Variations on a Winter Sunrise

I

A glacial sun at eight o'clock
Smears faint veneers in pastel chalk
Across a frigid strip of sky.
Heavy-coated, shivering, I
Walk toward the colors, down the block.

Across a frozen strip of sky,
Pale colors spread a tapestry
Behind the sun's white faceless clock.
Disfigured branches – crooked, dark –
Write cryptic script that draws my eye.

II

Beneath the winter sky's ice, purple-lipped,
I try to hurry the season along as I walk,
Reading between the lines of the branches' stark script
That foreshadows a cheerless nightfall before five o'clock.

Flashbacks of bushes that used to wear colorful clothes
Reflect my mental landscape as it thaws.
With lamenting admiration, I pass the rose
That has stayed here all winter. Briefly its icy coat glows.
My view is involuntarily drawn to the rows
Of windows – one on each side of the black-and-white block –
That reflect these naked trees, framed and enclosed
In illusions of warmth. One glass spreads orange glows
Of fireplace light; beside it, a grandfather clock
Has continued to tick through all changes of heat and snows,
Oblivious of the fire or the frozen rose.

III

This is the same route where
Perennials light up the year
When I pass by them wearing cooler clothes.
Now the cold trees wear
None – stark, bare,
Mirrored from these houses in their rows.

Thin, exposed branches
In inky skyline sketches
Of skeletal lines, are backed by dawn's warm colors
Which, drawn on the horizon,
Are erased as day keeps rising
And the landscape fades to winter's dull-gray pallor.

But this moment, daybreak glows
Behind wooden bones; it shows
More brightly when contrasted with their dark
Denuded branches, gaunt
Against the coral paint
Spread by a glacial sun at eight o'clock.

To the Rose that Stayed All Winter

"If to be warmed, then I must freeze
And quake in frigid purgatorial fires
Of which the flame is roses, and the smoke is briars."
— T.S. Eliot, *Four Quartets, (East Coker)*

"... And the fire and the rose are one."
— T.S. Eliot, *Four Quartets (Little Gidding)*

You, indomitable lady, refusing to be bent
By age, by disease, or anguish upon anguish,
By intolerable circumstances not mainly of your making –
Grasping life in spite of intractable winter, staking
Your stem against the belief that you were planted for a reason.
You exert yourself to express, in your voiceless but visible language,
Inexorable endurance: you still, you will, continue intent
On thriving among thorns, choosing as long as you breathe not to
    relinquish
Your relentlessly rooted stance. Your fragile frame nearly spent,
The flames of your red petals not yet extinguished,
You kept them warm against the cruel season's storms.

For you, Spring never came to stay.
Your life has been a cold blast of perennial taking away
Of pleasure rarely and falsely offered:
A treacherous charm under sparkling snow, a heat that warms
The sight, but harms the hand. All this, you strongly suffered.
You are this mute-tongued, frozen rose with paralyzed petals –
Still eccentrically red in the cold hard middle
Of February's sculptured-ice display,
Your color still fiercely protected by your brittle-
Boned, translucent-skinned breakable
Body. Beneath the snow, for the moment unshakable,
You clutch by tenacious

Intention whatever of life, by your unfathomable mind's estimation
Is salvageably good: the flower's curvaceous
Outline, still gracefully posed – your vindication
Of life: the resolute rose.

It would have been easier (everyone knows)
To fall gracefully, with the others, at autumn's end.
But this was your rejoinder to unkind life, your strong-willed choice
To keep your fire burning through darkness and ice.
You knew this winter was your last stand,
And last stands cannot come twice.
This one thing you required. a pure Spring day,
One uninterrupted moment of beauty, before you let your petals fall
    away.

Full Circle

"... And the end of all our exploring
Will be to arrive where we started
And know the place for the first time."
— T.S. Eliot, *Four Quartets: Little Gidding*

"That which has been is what will be;
That which is done is what will be done;
And there is nothing new under the sun."
— *Ecclesiastes 1:9* (NKJV)

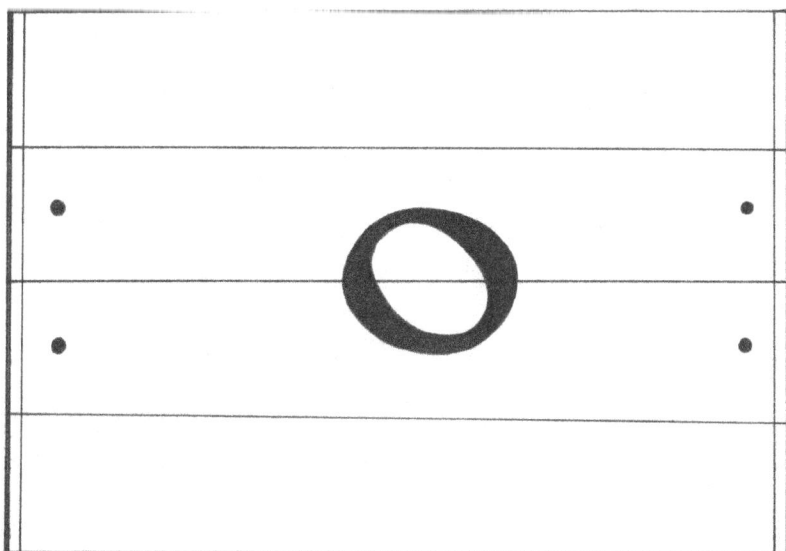

Michigan Exit, Highway 94: Homage to Michelangelo and T.S. Eliot

> "Shall I say, 'I have gone at dusk through narrow streets....?'"
> "In the room, the women come and go, talking of Michelangelo."
> —T.S. Eliot, "The Love Song of J. Alfred Prufrock"

I

Leaving in the cool of summer days
In June's long hours for well-arranged vacations,
We four have gone at first light into curving,
Nearly empty interstates, observing
The unseen artist's brushstrokes as he lays
Rising daylight's palette, spreads gradations
Of shiftingly-elusive pigmentations
Just above the highway's asphalt grays.
A masterpiece across the unframed skies,
"Freeway Entrance Just Before Sunrise"
Is painted on the canvas of the clouded
Ceiling of our scene. But hypnotizing
White stripes rush underneath our car; my eyes,
Distracted by them, miss the mesmerizing
Colors overhead, and soon they're muted.
     On the freeway, travelers pass, not tearing
     Their sights off dotted lane-lines, blankly staring.

II

We've rolled our universe into a room
On many one-night stays in chain hotels,
Then breakfasted in humdrum restaurants –

The syrup-scented early-morning haunts
Of overtired truckers who presume
To blend their nights and mornings with the smells
Of coffee, toast, and over-crispy bacon
Brought in by waitresses without a platter.
Where have they come from? What's their destination?
Do any ask the overwhelming question?
The scene outside the window doesn't matter;
The nondescript art scenes hung on the wall
Inspire no thought, leave minds insentient, dull.
The heavy blinds and lightweight idle chatter,
The ringing of the coffee cups and spoons,
Validate the tedium, won't waken
Desire to see a sunrise, or the moon's
Descent. All but routine is left unspoken.
    In the restaurant, workers earn their pay,
    While travelers leave their tips and drive away.

                        III

As afternoon approaches, three-toned skies
Of gauzy grays, weak blues, and drowsy whites
Above small towns appear to paralyze
Time's motions. Tired of sitting, restless, bored,
We spell things out of passing license plates,
Surprised at one that's made to say "Hes lord."
The landscape rushes by: a bright billboard
Calls "God is Love. Come worship with us." Piles
Of cumulus airbrush the sky's designs.
We drowsily pass by rural scenes and signs,
Try radio stations clouded by static, count miles.
    At sites and exits, tourists go and come,
    Unaware of signs of Christendom.

We yield to roadside ads for antique shops,
Suddenly round a circular exit ramp.
We find ourselves en-forested, and park
Beneath the greenery. Outside, we tramp
Through weeds and gravel, where the sound of cars
Seems quieter than the birds. Behind a copse,
Two buildings; as we're entering the first,
Our sun-glazed eyes adjusting to the dark,
We hear, as in a dream, the doorknob bell
Announce our entrance with a timid clink.
Cautious, standing still at first, we blink
Until our sight outlines the wood we smell,
And yellow-paged books, sweet with brittle age.
We read a while, sitting on two pews,
I musing how these books were but a page
Of history's drama acted on earth's stage.
We step into an art nook and peruse
Some stained-glass windows in which saints are kneeling.
"You'd like our chapel," the proprietor's
Voice intruded on our reverie.
"Our artist has depicted on the ceiling,
In oils, many Sistine Chapel figures,
Like the ones by Michelangelo.
If you like art, it's something you should see.
Do take a look at it before you go."
"Thank you – we will," I say, but skeptical.
The others glance at me: In Nowhere-ville?

V

The chapel's entrance is a plain glass door,
Just like a cafe or convenience store.
But to our shock – incongruously low,

Almost in reach – a stunning panorama
Of figures overhead retells a drama:
The ceiling is a canvas filled with life,
From God creating Adam and his wife
To Christ the Judge, all marked off in between
By ornate columns. Each bright-colored scene,
Though less ingenious than the true Sistine,
Gives energy to painted figures, grace
That keeps the head upturned, and lifts the spirit.
Far from the road, in this unlikely garret,
The final scene depicts the Risen Dead –
Unfinished. It is hard to tear our gaze
Away. We catch our breath, sit in a pew
And stare. Time seems to stop. I think how few
Will find this treasure. Can a thing this good
Come out of such a tiny niche in space?
My joy was dampened with a vague foreboding
Which did not leave me as we left the place –
This large world crowded into one small room –
To see earth's sky, our dazed ideas floating.
    Here we go round the ramp again,
    Outside of time, yet driving.
Now how, I wonder – how do we resume
Our certain spot in history and space,
In this uncertain hour of afternoon?
We have lingered in this chamber by the road
While traffic hurried by and our time slowed,
Not far from standing still; the still sky glowed.
Until this accidental, destined visit,
Have we mapped out our lives in hours and miles,
Replied to high designs with quick denials,
Refused to ask the universe, "What is it?"
Is what we thought we came for just the spoils
Of time away from work, for little whiles
Of lazy pleasure, warmth of June, or for
Mere tranquil entertainment – nothing more?

The settled mind that sees what it assumes,
Forgets the figured purpose as it looms
Like gusting clouds behind a garish billboard.
    On life's highway, we of narrow mind
    Continue driving, blind or mostly blind.

VI

This dreamlike episode was long ago –
A moment not in time but out of time.
One day this summer, coming from the place
We always come from, taking the same route,
But this time watching blurry rain erase
Celestial colors, suddenly without
Apparent evidence, we had a thought
That we were nearing Michelangelo.
Drawn by a goal we didn't know about,
Instinctively we circled the right ramp,
As if we'd heard a voice from that small room.
My unconfirmed foreboding that had stirred
When last we left the place, rose up: a feeling
Like blowing clouds of fast-approaching gloom,
Or fateful prophecies sketched on a ceiling.

The place was overgrown with weeds, and damp
With long disuse. What voice had we just heard?
The faded "Antiques" sign was still in place
Above the door; a broken table-lamp
And several kitchen gadgets at its base
Lay bleeding in a stagnant puddle – rust
Returning to earth's saturated dust.
Predestined thus, we walked without a word
Past delicately-boned and blossomed trees;
I felt that if I touched them, they would bleed.
With silent dread we moved like dripping ghosts,
Our sneakers soaked, across the gravel, toward
The chapel, barely visible through blurred,

Incessant drizzle.
                    Its glass doors were locked.
Remaining on the ceiling was one face:
An angel's singing silently transfigured
The chapel; still rejoicing with such grace,
We almost heard him sing as he extolled
His Maker.
                    All the other brilliant figures
Had disappeared beneath white paint. We gawked
A while, then turned dejectedly to grope
Our way back to the car. We felt expelled –
Yet not without a miniscule hope.

We have lingered in uncharted coves, where charms
Of beauty's vibrant treasures go unwanted,
Obscure artistic paradises, haunted
By visions that will vanish if unvaunted.
Should we have all been pairs of artists' arms
The brush across a ceiling? Had we heard
A voice, a calling, that we had ignored?
    Daily, yearly, travelers drive their routes,
    Unburdened by vocation, deaf to doubts.

Are we called to make revisions that security can't face?
In a lifetime there are visions that a rainfall can't erase.
Shall we not cease from taking the same route
In summertime, where we will likely find
Last summer's art is gone? Shall we begin
To look for what we think we've lost? Start over
Again? And if we do, will we discover
That we are loathe to bear the perilous cost
Of taking narrow side roads, getting lost?
    On life's highway, travelers rarely dare
    To lift their gaze, but only blankly stare.
Meanwhile, unbroken dawns and days extend:
The painted mornings, long-drawn afternoons,
And purple evenings with their musing moons

That wax and wane, reflecting on the end
From which we must begin, our destinations
Unknown.
        With new, unspoken speculations,
We scan the bending road and arching sky
Which offer only an oblique reply,
Unsettling us on well-arranged vacations.

Synchronicity

If lilacs could last till autumn's noon
Had draped their fragrance with its blooms
Of red and gold; if maple hues
Stayed bright beyond when snow assumes
The sparkle lent by winter's moon
At midnight; or if sunlit June
Could overlap its vivid views
With spring's new blossoms – such a dense
Display beneath the circling sun
Would overwhelm us, too intense
For eye and soul to take in at once.
Such saturate beauty we couldn't soak up;
Just one sight or scent at a time can stun
Our limited senses. Already our cup
Overflows, when the scent of the lilac blooms
Blends with our dread of their leaving that looms.
Soon we will stand under pre-solstice sun
Amid heady lilacs whose short life is done.

Perennial Parade

Fleeting flowers, passing fast –
Perfumed lilacs will not last;
Fully festive now, they cast
Their fragrance into May

As April's brightest yellows dull:
Aging forsythia sigh farewell
To daffodils, hunched, with brittling bowls,
Blonde dandelions gray.

Tree-blossoms – dogwood, redbud, cherry,
Magnolia magnificent and merry –
Drop petal-circles, as if to bury
Hyacinth's sachet.

Dormant since March, the crocus is laid
Beneath the new generation of shade,
Avoiding a view of the tulips that fade,
Evading our vague dismay

At the delicate beauty that is so brief,
Translucent as last autumn's threadbare leaf.
Early irises gush their grief
For the lilacs, browning away.

Meanwhile the evanescent azalea
Prevails over old rhododendrons' regalia,
Its burgeoning blossoms in bacchanalia,
Heralding the way

To the pageant of poppies and peonies,
Wielding sizeable scepters in tapestries
Of magenta and orange: bright novelties
Appearing in pompous display,

Flaunting their regal banners as though
Their competition for largest-in-show
Is indispensable to bestow
A laurel on the longest day.

But their kingdom soon falls, crowned lilies replacing
Their languishing landscape: kind monarchs, embracing
The air with benevolent essence, gracing
Our noses with brilliant bouquet,

And our inward ear with the reveilles
Of their silent trumpets' parade, while a breeze
Wreathes aromatic reveries
Around July like a lei.

No king is arrayed like one of these
Outlandishly lavish luxuries.
But the reign of their breathtaking revelries
Holds only transient sway

When honeysuckle's succulence
Exhales its singular incense.
Intoxicating, it prevents
Forebodings of Fall's decay

As, lifted from its leafy loom,
It dissipates all sense of doom,
Wafting its opulent perfume
Throughout the tent of sky.

But black-eyed susans' profusions, bold
In rows of sunlit August gold
Announce that summer is growing old.
Even sunflowers' light can't delay

The opening of the chrysanthemums,
Inaugurating autumn, which comes
With its own perennial, short-lived elations,
Delaying white winter with red jubilations.

Perennial Love

For Don and Faith, on the occasion of their
Fiftieth Wedding Anniversary

For fifty years, your love has glowed and grown,
A deeply-rooted plant in healthy soil.
Two-hundred seasons since, the seed was sown
In the mysterious time when, in between
The spring and summer, blooms lead out the green –
Bright blossoms fading as the leaves uncoil.
For every season has its secret toil
Beneath its glow: the scorching summer sun
Steals moisture while, invisible underground,
Roots struggle down to quench insistent thirst.
Green yields to autumn, whose fierce colors stun
The world with breathless beauty, and astound
With brazen-faced denial of the cursed
Approach of winter when the branches, bare,
Bereft of pulse and color, now look dead.
Then, only true and loyal love will dare
Have faith and wait for Spring, when branches don
Their blossoms once again. Thus are you wed:
Through heat and cold, through weather foul and fair,
A golden plant still flourishing and rare!

Late Bloomers' Lament

First, it's as if May's lilac – dormant till
The warmer months had laid themselves to rest –
Had kept its potent fragrance for the last
Festivity before the winter's blast,
Withholding blooms until the first of fall,
Then bursting purple with surprising zest.

And it's as if, with instinct too intense
To comprehend its reason for delay –
A curiously deep naivete –
Spring wished to catch the autumn unaware
With reminiscent, out-of-season scents
By perfuming the quickly-cooling air
While leaves are turning brown, and branches bare.

Then, it's as if a hostile early frost
Had fallen, just to taunt late-bloomers sent
To cheer the world, and thwart their warm intent,
Transforming it into a cold lament:
Each bloom wilts like a morning-glory's ghost;
Raw wintry winds delight to disenchant

Until – since spring and fall have never met –
The air is redolent of late regret.

Palms to Ashes

After the loud hosannas; past the psalms
From mouths of babes; beyond the shouted praise
Of unenlightened multitudes, the palms
That waved in jubilation one short day
Are left to start their gradual decay
From green to brittle brown. Through all the days
Of Holy Week, and weeks of Eastertide,
Forgotten with Lent's disciplines, they fade
Like short-lived fervor, cast aside and spurned,
No longer celebrated or displayed
Triumphantly, but stored till they are dried
By time and air and entropy, then burned.

Entombed in urns, the ashes wrap their gloom
Relentlessly around the year, extending
Their shadow toward Ash Wednesday's blackened ending,
As if it is our sure and certain doom
Subconsciously to know that Lent will loom.

Inexorably, their specter lengthens past
The seasons, though forgotten or unheeded
Until their crucial purpose is completed.
The flames of Pentecost cannot consume
Its subtle portent, nor can Advent's morning
Snuff out the coming darkness, or re-cast
The long approaching shadow of its warning.
It stretches on through Christmastide, and past
Ephipany, to join this Lent to last;
For gold and frankincense will not obscure
The ominous appearance of the myrrh
Which hovers over them, as ashes linger
From Lent to Lent, to mark us with decay
Which, since the Fall (although the grave delay)

Is written on us all with God's own finger.
For this portentous purpose they were saved:
For death's predestined deed to be engraved
Upon our foreheads, cruciform: a smear
Of old cremated palm leaves from last year.
From Eastertide until Epiphany,
We have denied our own mortality.
But with this somber rite, we'll be returned
To last year's Lenten lessons, still unlearned.

Ash-covered now, we know that we must grope
Through one more Lent, in sure and certain hope
That losses here will be transformed to gain,
And what cannot be burned will still remain.

Time Flies

"And the bird called, in response to
The unheard music hidden in the shrubbery."
— T.S. Eliot, *Four Quartets*

Anthem: Byrd in Flight

for the Choir of Mariners' Church of Detroit

"The better the voyce is, the meeter it is to honour and
serve God therewith: and the voyce of man is chiefly to
bee imployed to that ende."

— William Byrd

The surplice-vested, five-part choir,
Like sparrows on a five-tiered wire,
Gives flight to canticles of Byrd.
The flocks of lightweight, living notes
Ascend to where celestial thoughts
Send back their echo, and are heard
On earth because of William Byrd.

The varied voices that compose
The choir, in its ordered rows,
Reveal the meaning in the fence
Of notes on which, in music's words
Are written, winglike, William Byrd's
Profoundest thoughts and joyful sense
Of heaven's music's eloquence.

In complex patterns, feathered notes
Float ceiling-ward from singers' throats.
They hover there, and still are heard
While silently we pray, then file
Between the voices, up the aisle
Where earth and heaven are briefly blurred
In sacrament, communing while,
Miraculously, souls are stirred
And lift from earth with William Byrd.

The Falcon

"In what distant deeps or skies
Burnt the fire of thine eyes?
On what wings dare he aspire?
What the hand dare seize the fire?"
— William Blake, *The Tyger*

Falcon, falcon, flying high
Over pines that scrape the sky,
What ingenious deity
Has framed your feathers, formed your flight?

Who the head, and what the wings?
How the graceful hoverings,
The virtuoso circlings
That bate my breath, amaze my sight?

From pine to pine you glide with ease,
Then soar above the tallest trees
With widened wingspan in the breeze –
Dark silhouette in summer's light.

Where in the clouds' vicinity
Is he who gave such dignity
To you, but left humanity
Enslaved to gravity, in spite

Of having crowned him king of bird
And every beast? He gave his word
That man would rule; is it absurd
That on the sky's scroll you would write

With feathered pen, man's question why
God's image can't, like falcons, fly?

43

Where is his unseen eagle-eye
Who overrides this regal right?

Why did your maker choose to fashion
Mankind with such thwarted passion
For your lofty flight's elation:
Aching, craving to unite

With your unrestrained volition?
By his purposed prohibition,
We remain in adoration
Far below your lordly height.

Wounded fledglings, we are left
Of flight's facility bereft,
Helpless by our human heft,
Imprisoned in our grounded plight.

Did he who made mankind, make you?
And when he shall make all things new,
Will the zenith of your view
At last be our intense delight?

Airborne falcon, drawing high
Semicircles in the sky,
What artistic Deity
Has carved the pathway of your flight?

Robin on a Sculpted Stone

Robin on a sculpted stone
    all alone,
Why are you a welcome guest,
    brightly dressed
On this lawn of sorrow spread
    with the dead?
Isn't your unseemly song
    clearly wrong?
Inappropriate the note
    from your throat –
Here, atop a marker left
    by bereft
Parents who, with sorrow weighed,
    lately laid
Their beloved child to rest?
    If your nest
Should be visited by death,
    would your breath
Come less lively from your throat?
    would it float
In the proper minor key
    melody,
Fitting to accompany
    tragedy?

Yet your song is welcome here,
    and your cheer
Comforting, because you chant
    ignorant
Of the doom that spring denies.
    Harmonize,
For us, human misery's

     elegies
With the music you've conveyed
     in the shade
Of this weeping-willow air.
     Sing the prayer
We cannot express in words.
     Happy birds,
Chant your peaceful serenade
     when we're laid
Here for you to sing to us
     and we too
     are, like you,
Blessedly oblivious.

Not By Sight

"All your life an unattainable ecstasy has hovered just
beyond the grasp of your consciousness."
— C.S. Lewis, *The Problem of Pain*

Staring, straining my eyes, I fail to see
The embodiment of the music that I hear:
The cardinal's call, so clear, from somewhere near.
His notes, as brilliant as his blazing body,
Color the air, fly everywhere. But where is he?
Too small to see from here, too tall the tree
Where he poses, invisibly red, his crested head
Hidden.
          Enchanting bird, your call captivates, insists that I see –
Yet your spellbinding shape eludes me. Deign to delight
My vision: Take your flaming flight,
Convey your virtually visible voice
Here; land near my admiring face.
Something in me wants something of your grace,
Your avian elegance.
                    Avidly craving for Sight
And Sound to unite – to condense
Into one all-encompassing, consummate Sense –
I urgently scan the sky for a display of your brilliance.

                    But why this intense,
Unrelenting discontent with invisible joy? Why
The persistent fear that the bliss that seems so near –
The implication that I think I hear
In the music – might fly away
Before it is clear?
          If I could stare
From close enough to see your quills, would I
Be able to possess, with you, the sky?

47

Were you captive to my whim,
Obliged to be still at my will, would I acquire
Some of your weightless brightness? Could I escape,
By commanding your splendid shape, from
The heavy darkness of hopeless desire? Could I become,
Like you, serene, content to be somewhere between
The earth and sky,
If you were tied to my sight and never flew higher?
And would I, if I could, hold you here, in place,
As if joy could live as a captive voice?
                                        Yet let me send
My imagination with you, to attend
A continual concert. Show me from where it comes,
This mystifying music. Let it find
Its way into all of my senses – engulf my mind with hints
That echo all my wordless wants.
Grant me a transient glance
Of trancendent red that brings
Radiant inklings of permanent things
With invisible wings
That can't be guessed –
An ecstasy more muted than expressed.

Ventriloquist

Red bird, meant most of all to be seen,
Why do you hide in the evergreen?
You sing gleefully,
I look longingly –
Yet your scheme has often been
To throw your voice so I can't see
Your color in the needled tree.

Small bird, your large voice mocks my ear.
Why can't I see what I can hear?
You keep chanting
Without granting
An appearance. Do you jeer
At my futile beauty-hunting,
Haunting me with constant taunting?

Bright bird, for human view designed,
Your hide-and-seek is so unkind.
You tantalize
My straining eyes
By perching where I cannot find
You, but can only visualize
Your perfect shape and pleasing size.

Proud bird – among the green, a jewel
Of warmest red, yet coldly cruel –
Snugly pined,
You stay behind
Thick branches, while I play the fool
Searching for you, feeling blind
Where sight and sound should be combined.

Pert bird, you shake the branches twice,

Vexing me with your virtual vice.
Why must you veil
Yourself? Why fail
To incarnate your vivid voice?
Your form is fiery; but your soul,
If you could have one, would be cool.

Crowned bird, must my imagination
Suffice me for my admiration?
My steadfast quest
To see your crest,
In your conceited estimation,
Seems an arrogant request.
Yet I am your humble guest.

Quick bird, it is my lucky day:
At last, by chance, you mesmerize
Me with a brief view as you rise,
Hop forward for a moment's stay –
Then suddenly, headlong, realize
I've seen you – and you fly away.

Chaunticleer

"Seven times a day, dutifully, with a deep sense of their
importance, and by the immemorial command of the
Divine, Chaunticleer crowed his canonical crows."
— Walter Wangerin, *The Book of the Dun Cow*

At clockcrow, the rooster lordly escorts the dawn,
Draws it around again on his tail's train, blending
Its colors with the trail of another night's ending refrain.
He, asserting his sovereignty, solemnly struts
In liturgical pomp; his sharp chant cuts
Along the line where two days join remembrance
And expectation – where soil abuts
The sky's sun-dial face. Chiming Matins,
Timing Prime, he loudly lauds one more remarkable morning
Of ordinary time, granting it deep-rooted rhythm and rhyme
To accompany light's canonical climb.

The hours process with the sun – Tierce, Sext and Nones –
While, vain in his vestments (unweathered
By relentless seasons and days) he continues his crucial crowing
For work, and prayer, and rest when all is done.
The afternoon grays toward Vespers, each note feathered
With meaning, each measure of music bestowing
A wished-for word – distant, half-heard –
That voices the hidden harmony between
Yet-unseen hours and those that have already been,
                                        Foreshowing
Wrong things made right, gray things explained
In Time's cryptic idiom, eternally ordained.

Westminster Chimes

"All through this hour / Lord be my guide /
And by thy power / No foot shall slide."
— lyric inscribed in the Big Ben clock room

The sun begins to etch its arc of hours
Above the tower filled with bells that ring
The passing of the morning as a phrase
Of quarter-notes and dotted halves that fly
And float within this dome of earthly sounds.

Between the sundial-sky and churchyard grounds –
Where, deaf below their stones, named faithful lie –
Scores of soprano birds observe the days
As holy celebrations, echoing,
With quickened pulse, the music from the towers.

Each quarter hour
Echoes with praise,
Lending new power
To common days.

While bells resound,
While time goes by,
Each day is crowned
Like the noon sky.

The afternoon is circumscribed by sounds
From mouths of giant bells and tiny throats.
Winged notes ascend toward sunlight, blending bass
And treble tones, a harmony that tells
As only music can, that we belong
To both the earth and skies. The tower's song
Can raise us up in hope, as heavy bells
Send lightweight sounds toward heaven, a release

Of weighty expectation that will float
From depth of soul to height of sky, in rounds.

Summoned by bells
We, though earthbound,
Hear what time tells
Through their deep sound.

Should these be mute,
Without a doubt
Dead would salute,
Gravestones would shout.

With Evensong, time's circle closes. Gray,
In drawn-out decrescendo, drops its arc
And dims the solar halo that descends
At diminishing day. The cadence of the bells
Evokes time's mystery to those with ears
To hear some meaning in the tolling years.
Augmented by the brazen sound that swells,
The day resolves to its tonic; chiming ends,
The full moon's whole note shining in the dark:
The evening and the morning making day.

From north and south,
From west and east,
Out of their mouths
Bells have not ceased

To harmonize the seeming dissonance
Of days and hours that flail their finite wings
With time which is not our time: welcome hints
Of sunlight circling everything that sings

All
Through
This
Hour.

Between Times

"Between midnight and dawn, when the past is all deception
The future futureless, before the morning watch
When time stops and time is never ending;
And the ground swell, that is and was from the beginning,
Clangs
The bell."
— T.S. Eliot, *Four Quartets: The Dry Salvages*

Intersections

It smells and feels and sounds and looks as sweet
As earth's first morning, when the senses all
Combine to overwhelm: uncommon air,
Alive with fragrance, gentle on the skin;
Cool dewgrass blending with descending heat;
Anticipation merging with recall
As lilies open to release their rare
Aroma, replacing lilacs that have been
Already gone since May.

Few are these moments when perfections meet:
Flashback to spring, impeccable pre-Fall –
Foreshadowings of poignant places where
We see the line so thin
Between growth and decay –
Common and sublime –
Eternity and Time.

Midwinter Spring

"Midwinter spring is its own season."
-T.S. Eliot, *Four Quartets: Little Gidding*

Winter and Spring – as a rule, mortal enemies –
For this one otherworldly, last day of January,
Have blended as friends, suspended in harmony,
Holding in tension the rare and the ordinary.
All night from a hidden place, a lyrical breeze,
Leftover at dawn, liquified the snowscape's freeze.
This morning it blew melted ice into murmuring drains
Along with the liquid remains of the snowbud corsages
Dropped from the colorless branches, where avian choirs
Rehearsed with the passion spontaneous spring inspires.
Outside the library in wet afternoon
An impromptu duet, clarinet and bassoon,
Accompanies the birds' elevated tune. On the lawn
Bicycles – abruptly freed from their idle garages –
Make muddy trenches, crudely drawn
With deflated tires. On barely-dried benches,
Below the branches that serve as the singers' risers,
Damp boots dangle near thin-crusted puddles
That quietly crack as the weird warmth settles.
Readers with open books and open coats
Listen and look, forget what's on the pages,
Shivering with alien heat,
Their souls' sap quivering like the just-melted water
That trembles under fragile ice-shields, gurgles in the gutter.
The scrapbook-page landscape recalls third-grade
Art class: crude collages we made
Out of random slick-paper scenes
We cut with blunt scissors from old magazines
And sealed with little ponds of glue

On bright construction paper (long ago turned gray
And brittle.) Many of these will stay
In mothers' memory boxes, just as Today –
This blurred watercolor – won't fade away
From our minds' pages. Hurriedly, it has merged
The unlikely with Now, its dreamlike incongruity urging
Our suddenly-unwintered senses to silently surge
In this stillpoint before the refreeze tomorrow.
Fused here at this moment with this eccentric day
We catch our breath, exhilarated to borrow
From Spring – to breathe its magic, smell its marrow.

The Moment of Our Lord

Now earth stands still; now time hangs weighted
With expectant thrill, its cadence suspended:
A cosmic clock's anticipated
Pendulum swing has stopped between
B.C. and A.D. At the top of its arc,
Like a wrecking ball in history's fading dark,
It is poised to demolish the era that has ended –
Yet with hardly a sound, scarcely heard or seen
By the world, whose temporal rhythmic gears
Could not have told its minutes or counted its years.
Here, past and future are quietly invaded
By this present moment. Earth's old timepiece is outdated,
Replaced by the gift of eternal meaning
From One who ever shall be, and who was from the beginning.

Organic Recital Invitation

Organ Recitals, Thursdays in Advent — All are welcome.
— Banner outside of Mariners' Church of Detroit

Come in and hear, all you who pass
Through urban noise
Against cold wind that beats your ears
And deafens thought –
For whom this place of stone and glass
Has been a landmark on your route,
An unread note for days, an unheard voice
For weeks or years.

If you are blown about and tossed
Like yesterday's
Discarded papers – driven, carried
Through life's maze,
Whirling past while feeling lost
And winded – or you've wondered what
Might be the meaning in your hurried
Ways, do not –

Just for today – do not rush past.
Come in and still
Your breathless haste.
Come in with your subconscious query.
Come in, and feel
A warmer wind above your hurry.
Pause, and breathe
An air where chaos doesn't seethe.
Take a timeless moment's rest.
Enter here, and be a guest
Of royalty – let music's King's

Respiring breath reveal a vast,
Invisible sphere.
Relax your labored lungs, and hear
Overtones of otherworldly things.

Stairway to Heaven: "The Dorian"

— for Kevin Bylsma

"Then [Jacob] dreamed, and behold, a ladder was set up on the earth, and its top reached to heaven; and there the angels of God were ascending and descending on it."

— Genesis 28: 12 (NKJV)

Prepared to scale the mind of Bach,
The organist begins his climb
Up out of ordinary time
Beyond the calendar and clock.

The steps up to his loft (which floats
Between two worlds, an octave higher
Than earthbound thought) lead to a choir
Of pipes that breathe seraphic notes.

His hands and feet become like wings,
Ascending and descending on
A stairway made of sound that sings,
From laddered keyboards, Dorian
Translations of the lexicon
Of angels: hopeful echoings
Half-heard, half-known by mortal men,
That speak to us of everything.

Thus at the topmost stair suspended
In this lofty atmosphere,
As in a dream, we briefly hear
Heaven's songs to us descended.

March 21st, Saints Cranmer and Bach

Archbishop Thomas Cranmer, burned at the stake
March 21, 1556
Johann Sebastian Bach, born March 21, 1685

"Upon them hath the light shined." — Isaiah 9: 2

The shadows of two saints come to my mind
As smoke from two extinguished candles rises
To end the service on this twenty-first
Of March. I visualize their smoke entwined:

The crackling flames that climaxed Cranmer's crisis
Were music to the men who thought him cursed –
Poetic justice (at his martyrdom,
He claimed his death would light the earth.) But from
His rhythmic prayers, a fireproof book has come,
And burned into the Church's memory
Its common prayer of lyric liturgy
That keeps igniting worship, as it kindles
Our faith, rising like smoke from altar candles.

To bring to birth his never-dying work,
Bach often had to write his masterpieces
By candlelight, with insufficient rest
From grueling days. Composing after dark –
Soli Deo Gloria – his Masses,
Celestial chorales for earthly choirs,
Concerti, anthems, fugues, he penned his vast
And everliving corpus that expresses,
In prayerful music, unextinguished fires.

Like flames, their words and music light the dark.
Pray for us, Saint Cranmer and Saint Bach.

Ascension Day: Facing East

"Between the essence and the descent
Falls the shadow."
— T.S. Eliot, *The Hollow Men*

"... All things proceed to a joyful consummation."
— T.S. Eliot, *Murder in the Cathedral*

The candles lit, the altar boys
Assume their seats. The smoke ascends.
The incense, in procession, tries
To lift our prayers. Its climbing lends
Assistance to the paltry praise
With which offenders make amends.

The crucifer with graceful poise
Hoists up the cross. The choir blends
With organ's breath. All voices rise.
The thurifer in reverence bends
To God who, from on high, surveys
The fallen hearts of those he tends.

The people kneel and raise the voice
Of common prayer. The priest extends
The bread and wine of sacrifice.
We elevate our hearts, and sense
Impending Pentecostal days,
Expectant with exuberance.

Retort to George Gordon, Lord Byron:

Stanzas Written Looking Back Down the Road of Youth and Age

O, do not recall to me revels of youth,
When roaring hormones blinded us to much truth;
When we thought we knew all, but knew little beside
Our feelings, our wants, the demands of our pride.

At twenty, when none was allowed to advise us,
Our fancied omniscience inclined us to choices
We made for their semblance of love and of glory,
Increasing their sound and inflating their fury.

The mantle of myrtle has mercifully paled;
The narcissus and poppy are ceding the field
To the wisdom of iris, the violets' humility
And the carnation's pink token of constancy.

The early wildflowers of youthful emotion,
So short-lived and shallow, with shifting devotion,
Bloom fast, but soon pale, making way for calm age
To yield ripening love like a garland of sage.

Youth's garden is bright, but its weeds soon grow wild;
In time, if well-kept, mature soil will yield
A flourishing plant with a deep-rooted story.
The days of our age may be lavish with glory.

Transition Times

"...If the present were always present and did not go by into the past, it would not be time at all, but eternity."

— St. Augustine, *Confessions*

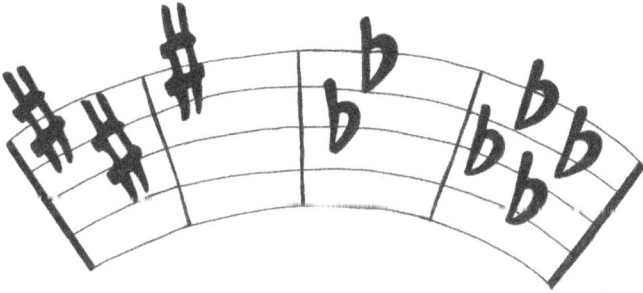

Transition Time

This is the time when plenty comes
But nothing stays:
When blackeyed susans are losing their rays
Of gold, while fences of folding hibiscus become less dense
With pink. On the brink of dropping their final blooms, they yield
To September's chrysanthemums, soon revealed
As Autumn's sovereigns, staving off cold with burnt orange and gold.

Ghostlike, post-August heat extends its stillness, suspending
Its embers beyond the border of seasonal order, and sends
Its fading waves over homes and graves, blending
Its warmth with September's colors.

Towering sunflowers, once nearly connecting
With the hot day-star they've been reflecting,
Turn their crowned heads toward the ground, elderly, bending,
Conceding their kingdom's end, resigning
As the image they mirror surrenders
To shorter days.

Meanwhile, ubiquitous roses have quietly dropped their blooms, designing
A dazzling red-petal pattern on green, seldom seen,
That reflects the breeze-rattled tambourine leaves overhead
That are turning with startling speed from green to red.

Quickly now comes the time
When all brilliant things will pass.
Few colors will be staying;
Warm scenery is graying;
Chilly changes will be blowing
While barren branches cast
Their no-longer-glowing leaves on grass

Still in its prime
Until first frost
When long daylight will be lost,
When all coming will be going
And the trees stand stark
As the season's pulse is slowing
And any secret growing
Will be done in the dark.

Late Bloomers

My last red rose-of-sharon
    Is slowly curling closed,
Each giant shell-shaped petal
    Beginning to turn in,
The five of them a pinwheel,
    Crepe-paper veins exposed
To August's reminiscence
    Of the summer that has been.

Today it holds its brightness;
    Tomorrow it will fall –
Frail, old, already rotting,
    After one dazzling day
Of reigning in the garden,
    Crowned king by size, like Saul –
And lie unburied on the grass
    With others, and decay.

Huge five-point blossoms, meanwhile,
    Herald the pumpkin, queen
Of autumn's golden garden.
    Their vines like giants' veins
Have overlapped the chainlink fence
    To tangle in between
Two yards, to join two seasons
    At the seam where summer wanes.

They weave the raveled sentiments
    Of August and September,
Portending things we almost know
    But never quite remember.

Fall Back: Central Standard Time

Already it is dark: the falling arc
Of each advancing year, when the eager moon,
To catch the setting sun, comes up too soon.
Full light no longer lingers at high noon,
Or loiters there long past our long day's work,
But languishes at waning afternoon:
Sunset's at six, then five, then four o'clock.

The day appears to finish prematurely;
We're turning kitchen lights on much too early.
The hour is young; the sun, about to swoon,
Has barely time – because of earth's strange quirk
Of turning on its oddly-tilted axis –
To paint the sky its customary pink
Before we look outside, before we think
About how long ago the summer solstice
Extended day. Now, waking in the dark,
We know this year is wholly past its prime:
We've fallen back to Central Standard Time.

Cutting Down Chrysanthemums

"What we call the beginning is often the end
And to make an end is to make a beginning.
The end is where we start from."
— T.S. Eliot, *Four Quartets*

The end is where we start from. This last chore
Of Autumn must be done. I have delayed
To lay to rest these brilliant colors for
Too long, till they've had time to wilt and fade.
Enamoured of their long-lived orange fire
That flames long past the burning bush's red,
I've left them to transform into a bier
Revealing Fall's rich revels to be dead.
But as the cold and darkness spread their pall
On earth and air, another season spreads
Its warmth: the Advent wreath's first candle sheds
A single flame that quivers on the wall.
The orange blooms of Fall have dropped their rays
And passed the flame to Advent's purple blaze.

Rondel for a Passing Year

Autumn's flaming color scheme has faded;
Dusk has smothered shortened day's last ember.
Can the brown chrysanthemums remember
When their blazing hues became outdated?

Last month's lawn was jewel-green brocaded
Tapestry inlaid with red and amber:
Autumn's flaming color scheme unfaded.
Now, dusk has smothered shortened day's last ember.

Days ago two seasons, still conflated,
Layered warmth with cold like gold and umber
Leaves that overlap: a last belated
Prelude to a colorless November.
Autumn's flaming color scheme has faded;
Dusk has smothered shortened day's last ember.

Waiting

I. Foreboding

The ground is bleeding maple-red. Its wound
Already has been covered with a gauze
Of late November's quickly-scabbing frost
To heal the gash, but not its chronic cause.
Stark-limbed, its former glory on the ground,
A bloodless skeleton looks down   a ghost
Of all the blazing splendor it has lost –
Content to stand at his appointed post,
Resigned to look decrepit, pale and old,
And wait till warmth prevails and cold
Is no more found.

II. Anticipation

Islands of grass in the melting snow,
Ponds of shadow amid the glow
Of March's puddle of early light:
Here, thin-limbed, aged trees still wait
To be re-clothed as they were dressed
A year ago, in infant white.
Meanwhile, they cast a shaded nest
Of slender branches on the bright
Expectant white-green blend
Of winter's end.

Six-Month Sonatina

November is the lengthening shade of age –
    A shrouded fright:
Lusterless grass clings to earth's frosty scalp,
    Prelude to dreaded white.
Monochrome gray begins its ominous spread
    Across an ageless sky
While tenor breezes sing notes that have started to slide
    Slightly off-key.
Deception dances through the head;
    Selective perception's charm
Sings fancies that exclude all dread
    Or omens of alarm.

May is the timeless moment of youth's delusion:
    Euphoric, furious –
Dense blossoms intoxicate with fragrant confusion:
    Heady, delirious.
A giddy dream's half-hidden imagination
    Dressed up as eternal Today
Asserts in the season's alluringly colorful fashion
    That its ecstasy will stay.
Oblivious to blossoms furtively descending
    Like disturbing dissonant notes,
We refuse to hear the cadence of Spring's ending,
    Transposing all minor-key thoughts.

We cannot change how time transforms,
With sun and storms, each season's expected refrains
Nor where it signs its strange designs, nor what it means
When its signature suddenly changes – abruptly declines
To remain, for the length of a tune, in a major key –
Or, like Autumn's decrescendo, chromatically
Fades from festive orange to muddy grays.

Rhythm becomes unpredictable: capricious measures,
Unfinished phrases, ungainly rhymes,
Erratic lyrics, haphazard melodies,
And unresolved dissonances undermine
The elusive pursuit of a harmony we can rely on –
Our subconscious illusion of holding the world's baton.

Autumn Next After Commencement

Papery leaves quiver above us in afternoon blazes,
Fall around our past and our present in shaded, evocative phrases:
Double-exposed Octobers of campus colors commence
To drift and descend in verses of cursive spirals, to spell
Rhythmic syllables and whisper words of favorite bards, overwhelming
    all senses
With seasonal stanzas charged with God's Grandeur[1] again.

Flaming maple and reddening apple frame the scene;
Yellowing pear images lines of Augustine; the chapel bell
Peals Westminster Chimes, juxtaposes
Last year with now. The lingering roses'
Sudden scent summons remembered insights, uncovers forgotten
    discoveries –
Momentary mental home-comings – while
Tambourine aspens shake their surprising
Percussive cymbals, symbolizing
Our quickening heartbeats, exciting souls with a breeze
Of Spenser's sonnets or Shakespeare's soliloquies.

Tremulous limbs shiver with drying remnants
Of nature's parchment, recalling
Offbeat Marianne Moore and dotted-note drummings
Of lower-case cummings.
Elderly willows still clap their staccato Ode to the West Wind,[2]
Whose shadows long have rolled
With a mighty meaning of a kind
That tells the more the more it is not told.[3]

---

[1] Gerard Manley Hopkins
[2] Percy Bysshe Shelley
[3] Edwin Arlington Robinson, "The Sheaves"

In intriguing tempos they drop their muted gold
To the Leaves-of-Grass[4] canvas world, their syncopated
Cadences and dense designs fusing music with visual art
On paths we walked before we graduated. Underfoot,
Unshaded, sunburnt umber oak leaves crunch percussively, waking
Echoes of passionate Browning passages, quaking with the quality
Of Blake's cryptic messages, evoking
Wordless versions of Wordsworth's Intimations of Immortality.[5]

Bright orange bittersweet and haunting Auden
Audibly echo last Autumn's garden;
Aging auburn leaves smell
Like old books on library shelves that swell
With Herbert, Hopkins, Hardy, Chesterton.
Behind red brick that the word-painter Betjeman
Called less intensely red than hawthorn berries,[6]
Its vivid ivied walls house Housman, Hawthorne, Dante, Donne.
In the changing air there is
Foreshadowing of first frost;
The blown-about birches and beeches are tossed
In musical movements that kindle thoughts of Millay's
Aged orchards that still bear and blaze.[7]

Yellowed elm and vintage pages of Eliot swell the spirit, alert our finite
  sense
To timeless moments'[8] immense significance,
Overwhelm it with intense fragrance
Of potent rose petals, densely-layered against the grass, still fresh,
Aflame: rust-bordered but not yet turned to ash.

---

[4] Walt Whitman
[5] William Wordsworth
[6] John Betjeman, "Autumn 1964"
[7] Edna St. Vincent Millay, "If Still Your Orchards Bear"
[8] T.S. Eliot, "Four Quartets"

Cooler autumn elements release their choice incense,
Blending with unheard melodies sweeter[9]
For their capricious meter.
This year's last red, ready to burst into lyrical laughter
(Hidden in the burning bushes) exalts the Fall
With inscaped energy of All-Saints' chants,
As if downwhirling leaves could rise in descants
Instead of descending.
We revel in these, although knowing what comes after
This seasons' bliss: already, brittle branches abound among
Grounded leaves and those, still hung
On boughs, that pluck the strings of the breeze
Till it moans like an athlete dying young.[10]
Its minor-key overtones harmonize
With a cold gust reminiscent of Gray's[11]
Eloquent elegy – a lamenting phrase
Of which resolves in a dirge for the ending
Of color and all that encourages ecstasy –
Implying, alluding – not shallowly telling –
That nothing gold can stay.[12]

Yet in the sunlit chapel, stonework soars and springs
To fountain out a spreading vault, a shower that never falls.[13]
Unfading stained-glass charged with immortal meaning
Pulses with potent light, profoundly adorning
Wood, stone, trees, air –
Makes beating hearts more fully aware
Of the one true permanence,
Wakes every solemnly jubilant sense
To the summoning bell's warning
That this life and its death will pass
And new life commence.

---

[9] John Keats, "Ode on a Grecian Urn"
[10] A.E. Housman, "To an Athlete Dying Young"
[11] Thomas Gray, "Elegy Written in a Country Churchyard"
[12] Robert Frost
[13] John Betjeman, "Sunday Morning, Kings' Cambridge"

Reminiscence

How must you face the tyranny of rude,
Encroaching final winter that invades
A mind once so alive? Its claims intrude
As autumn's deep green grasses change their shades,
On earth's cold scalp, to sickly sage and gray.
When late November's features crack and pale,
You must relive your life's remembered May,
Where songs and dances bloom and never fail.
No winter's nightmare will you let reveal
The false notes that your sweet deception sings;
But on today's dead blooms, you spread a pall
Of daydreams with their cavalcade of springs.
When time exposes minds to cold decay,
They must relive the warmth of yesterday.

Diamond Anniversary:
For Better, For Worse

His

You are the husband, and you are the nurse
While other nurses tend to other patients.
You feed her breakfast with painstaking patience,
Accepting selflessly your loneliness.
You fed her wedding cake this summer day
Six decades since, and promised to be true.
You have been. She's been faithful to you, too.
Today you bring a fragrant rose bouquet.
She pays it no attention, turns away,
Does not remember when you said "I do"
To one another. Now she wonders who
You are sometimes, though you don't miss a day
Of filling most of your exhausting hours
With wheeling her outside to see the flowers,
And feeding her, and reading to her, while
She hears or doesn't hear. Your soul is mourning
The loss of her companionship, her smile.
Each day you say it, but there's no good morning
(Since not your wounds, nor hers, have hope of healing.)
And sadness couples with fatigue at night;
You kiss her gently; she stares at the ceiling.
Your sleep feels brief; too soon returns the light.

Hers

There's nothing left to talk about. The life
You've known is gone. This running trophy, won
At your last race (twelve years ago) was one
Of many, but now poses by herself,

Your diamond ring on her arm, on this small shelf,
Beside you in your wheelchair. Once you ran
Five miles a day; and so did this kind man
Who coached and cheered for you. You've been his wife
For sixty years. He speaks, but you are dumb.
He lifts food to your mouth; you only chew.
He holds a wedding picture up for you,
But you don't seem to know these people from
The other patients here. In fact, you close
Your eyes (against the thought that you're a burden?)
Since, all those years ago, he gave his word in
The sight of God and witnesses, he does
These loving things. Though you, too, made that vow,
It benefits your husband nothing now.
Is this what you are thinking, why you're not talking?
Can't you – or won't you? Do you feel life mocking
Your helplessness, and feel the brutal curse
Of being the Worse in "for better or for worse"?

Time Signatures:
Elegy on the Hymn "St. Anne"

"A thousand ages in thy sight are like an evening gone."
— Isaac Watts

I

The funeral service was the easy part,
compared to what came after: cleaning house,
deciding what to keep or throw away.
Where does one even start to sort, when they
still seem to be here with us, echoing
our voices and our feelings?
                              Shall we store
the name-plaque we had given them one spring,
securely mounted now at the front door?
The birthday card, still standing on the little
end table by the sofa, that all four
of us had signed? The loose-paged, well-used hymnal,
open on the piano – yellow, brittle,
its incense rising like a silent prayer:
"O God our help in ages past" displayed,
Which only last week she had likely played?

II

The clock bequeathed to me chimed half-past two;
We looked around at all we had to do.
It seemed that this should take a thousand ages;
A life should not be quickly swept from sight:
The photo albums with their fragile pages,

some pictures falling out, some empty spaces,
some well-remembered, and some unknown, faces;
a box of birthday / get-well / Christmas cards;
a plaque engraved to dad with THIRTY YEARS
OF SERVICE; stacks of childhood awards
of ours that mom preserved; my brother's bears.

III

I found my autograph book in the closet
(I never thought, back then, I'd ever lose it)
bought at the five-and-dime when I was ten
or so – its polka-dotted, black-and-white
Existence long-forgotten, as my dream
to meet the baseball player, whose signed name
would not have ever crossed my mind again.
Short as the fad that ends a childhood's flight
of fancy, home runs fly from memory.
The other pages all were blank. The sight
that flashes back is mother on my right,
dad on my left, indulging my young whim
To stand close to the gate and wait for him.

IV

A will is such a dreadful thing to sign,
I thought, reading my parents' names, cross-stitched
above their wedding date. (Who would take home
This heirloom which had hung here in the hall
Making its mark upon the faded wall
Since they had moved in – newlyweds, well-matched?)
This wedding gift received its silver frame
Before we were. Its worth would be the same
For each of us.
                    I thought of Grandma Anne

Cross-stitching each of us a graduation
Memento, and remembered my name scratched
By her, with a big branch, into a new
Clean page of sunlit snow one Christmas vacation.
My own name, sparkling like diamonds! I said, "I do!"
When she asked me if I liked it.
                              Half-past nine.
I only half-heard it, shivering now from that time
In the snow, which had seemed more real at this moment than
Being here, where I felt like an actor in pantomime.

                    V

A dozen boxes filled, an evening gone.
"Our lives," my sister said, just as we heard
The clock chime half-past ten, "are half-completed."
"Some day," our brother started – then retreated.
Time bears its sons and daughters all away;
Yet for a while, sons and daughters stay
To sort through artifacts of yesterday.
I pocketed dad's favorite fountain pen
With which he'd written cursive rolling streams
Of letters to us and our progeny;
They flowed on tides of magic postal air
(His favorite form of high technology).
And what will they (our progeny) inherit
From us? What words that haven't been deleted
From cyberspace – forgotten, as the dreams
That disappear, as if one's memory's garret
Has no more megabytes on which to store it?
Will grandpa's box of letters be a burden
To them, an added clutter to their closet?
Will ours be the forgotten generation,
With civilization going paperless?
Does paper serve a vital purpose? Does it

Preserve descendants' hopes for years to come –
Bring help from ages past into their homes –
A link for future children to possess?

VI

"We'd better stop," our youngest sister said –
Her eyes, like ours, glazed like the cellophane
In photo albums, but red with mourning rain.
She picked up mom's gold watch. Short is the night.
"It's midnight. We're dead-tired. Let's go to bed."
I looked to see if anyone else might
Have caught her unintended morbid pun.
The spell of memories broke, and then the ache
Returned. At this point, none of us would wake
Before the rising sun.

VII

Ignoring the mirror behind my old dresser, I gaze
At my photo of them, and reflect on how much it seems
That life is continually falling apart at the seams.
In a stupor, I stare at the patch of the quilt that's been mended
Many times, and is torn again where my sister's name
Is embroidered, with her birth date. The quilt was designed
By one who is no longer living – mom's best friend.
It had a square for each of us: a scheme
Of squares in a circle, our cursive names expanded
Around the circumference like an ornate frame
As if we had signed a pact, our signatures joined.
I carefully crawled beneath it in a daze,
Being careful not to touch the loosened threads.

VIII

Under the shadow of our life's new phase
("We are the old ones now," mom once had said
After Grandma had died), sleep was a haze
Of waking dreams and thinly-clouded dread
That wakefulness would end this swatch of the night
Before I could bear the ruthless rising sun.
They'd been our help in ages past; now we
Must be the shelter – be strong to display,
For our sons and daughters, assurance even when
All hope has seemed to vanish from our sight.
Subconsciously, I'd always felt secure
When I could take for granted parents were
Still with us. Now that we've come to this day,
It feels like we're drowning in time's waterfall
That's destined to bear all of us away.

IX

I startled awake to the shrill alarm that sliced
My haunted dream at break of daunting day.
At once I wished my dream could fly away,
Forgotten, with its stalking memories:
Our history of family conflicts, voiced
In sublimated nightmares. Now that she's
Not with us, will these ever-rolling streams
Bear voluntary silences away?
Is there a shelter from the stormy past?
A thousand pages, if these walls could write
Our story on themselves, perhaps could cast
It as a novel filled with tragic themes
Belying happy smiles and gilded frames,
And plague us all with sleepless nights
And endless years of blame.

Yet all our happiest
Remembrances will also make their claims
In dreams outside (as we are now) of time.

X

Dreams dying at the opening of day,
We took down family photos, still in frames;
Slipped others out of useless album pages
Whose faded captions whispered long-lost names,
Forewarning us of memory's decay
That steals perniciously in subtle stages.
Before this house in brick and order stood –
Before its floors were laid; before its wood
Was cut; before its builders made its frame –
The two of them spoke one another's names
And vowed that through their lives they would endure
Together, giving shelter through life's blast:
Always her life for him, his life for her
As long as fickle earthly breath would last
Till, side by side their names, now etched in stone,
Give witness to the truth that they were one.
As they'd engraved themselves upon our lives,
So through the stormy blast, their love survives.

XI

They'd both outlived their threescore years and ten;
And, yes – their last years' strength was loss and sorrow.
And now we wonder: how long till our own
Remembrances subside into the shadow?
This, too, is nothing new beneath the sun:
When all that one has thought and said and done,
In body and in mind, is just an ember
Of all we ever were or wished to be.

We've no desire to learn – yet must – to number
Our days, instead, desiring to be free
To go back and pursue our urgent plan,
Resuming next week where last week began.

XII

We'd weathered the qualm I'd had before death's storm,
And so this loss had made its own bequest:
Our family's bond was stronger than I had guessed.
And now, mom's stacks of calendars that I'd buried
In their brittle box, when the garden's ground turned warm,
(The oldest one was from the year they'd married)
Are fertilizing lilies that may last
Beyond our own lives' sun and stormy blast,
And make from all the days' and decades' loam
A fragrant prayer for our eternal home.

Out of Time

"Time and the bell have buried the day,
The black cloud carries the sun away."
— T.S. Eliot, *Four Quartets: Burnt Norton*

"In the Midst of Life We are in Death."

— The *Book of Common Prayer*, The Order for The Burial of the Dead

In sure and certain hope, we toss
The soil in, and bless the dead.
The final sentences; that pause
Of awkward length, when all our breath,
Suspended, makes a short-lived sheath
Around the dead, and we bequeath
To this one all we have, our grief.
And then we must, with reverent tread,
Unsteady, turn and step across
The shadow of our silent dread
Of going back where we must breathe,
Once more, the air of common earth –
As if we have not been away,
Inside another kind of day:
A dreamlike time when we're awake
To other worlds. Out of the deep,
Against death's flow, we undertake
To surface from a stormy sleep.

The last insulting sting of death
Is not that dust returns to dust
But that, like Lazarus, we must
Return, unwilling, with a veil
Between us and this world – a place
Which recently had seemed quite real –
And never be the same, and face
Unsurely, for uncertain length
Of time, our lives, deprived of strength.

And then the brutal car doors close.
They slice the silence, break the spell

(Although emotion's waves still swell
And heave beneath our mourning clothes),
As our attempts to breathe the air
Of both worlds – gasping as we are –
Inevitably fail. Banal
Details rip through our thoughts' thick pall,
Abruptly force a change of gear
That dulls the day's significance –
Loose gravel underneath the car;
Our seatbelts clicking as we glance
To catch a last look in the rear-
View mirror. Traffic – trite, mundane,
Oblivious – rolls past the lawn
Of gravestones where we just have been
(And somehow feel we still are there).
Stoplights and work-zone signs and rain
Engulf us. Easy silence gone,
Permission not to speak withdrawn,
Makes one of us suggest in vain
A drive-thru coffee for our pain.

Burial Office: Sunset

"So did the world from the first hour decay,
That evening was beginning of the day.... "
— John Donne, *The Anniversaries: An*
Anatomy of the World

While beauty's noon consumes away;
While sunset colors fade and die;
While evening hours begin another day
With only light and dark to measure by –

Let not your heart be troubled. Think
Of calendars and coffee pots,
And not of how your world is on the brink
Of breakdown as its crumbling center rots.

Ignore earth's image of your end,
And disregard the death of Day.
From it, make no attempt to comprehend
The universal nature of decay.

Evade the vision – block all view
Of Daylight's casket lowered in.
Suppress this stark reflection of a clue
To humans' short-lived threescore years and ten.

Where midnight masquerades as dawn,
And morning ends the seventh day;
Where memory's fragile ashes soon are gone,
And twilight's dust goes out an unseen way,

Take no heed to dark's intrusion.
Seek the trivial. Count no cost.
Avoid night's unavoidable conclusion
Till evening's partial light is wholly lost.

Corpse

unkempt weeds decay
    on the scalp of the gutted house
bloodless wisteria veins wind
    around its rotting ribs
dead leaves dampen
    the living room's diaphragm
the grandfather clock has stopped beating
the potbellied stove is empty
smaller viscera decompose
    inside the cedar chest
but the translucent curtains weakly inhale
and expire earth's ancient dusty dirge.

Death in Spring

On the Second Saturday after Good Friday,
Returning from Evening Prayer,
I received a stark impression:
All my senses were aware
Of a virtual hole in what had been
Easter-scented air.

The wide, white-blossomed pear tree
In all her bridal bloom
Whose fragrance had eastered my spirits
Just this afternoon
Had disappeared completely,
Leaving only gloom:

A patch of empty sky
For yesterday's bouquet,
And a circular sawdust pall
Beneath it on the clay –
A small heap of eraser dust,
Belying the life of May.

September Cemeteryscape

Daybreak's darkness dissipates:
　　Glow-through leaves are yellowing;
　　Chiseled names, in dawn's first rays,
　　Are legible. Old willows sing
　　With breezy voice, in cryptic phrase.

Splashing sunlight saturates
　　Diamond-dew-and-emerald lawn,
　　Ray-reflecting marbled stones.
　　Light-edged leaves in brassy dawn
　　Shake; the last cicada drones.

Liquid light illuminates
　　The fountain's arching silver spray
　　While oak-umbrellas, green since May,
　　Signify, above these rocks,
　　The buried-acorn paradox.

Shortening shadows undulate
　　Across the blinding glassy sheen
　　That mirrors light from dark-veined stones
　　Spread out here like a city scene.
　　In brightening, deceptive tones,

Autumn's augurings augment
　　The harmonies of rhythmic red
　　And descant-orange leaves, intense
　　With echoes of the same things said
　　Last year, but in the future tense.

Music's meaning mediates:
　　The leaves' percussion overhead
　　Is blended with the woodwinds: birds

Repeat their themes above the dead:
Exquisitely unearthly words

Whose shrouded meanings can't be found
    Below this canopy of sound
    Since humans' loss of heaven's tongue
    In Eden, where we might have sung

Perpetually in perfect state
Which death could not obliterate.

Requiem

"Till we have built Jerusalem In England's green and pleasant land."

— William Blake

"And the Church must be forever building, and always decaying, and always being restored."

— T.S. Eliot, Choruses from *The Rock*

Three headstones: one marked "Love," one "Everlove,"
And one – cathedralesque in ancient time,
Now cracked and leaning as if it would fall,
Marked "England" – cast their autumn evening's pall
Of blended shadow shaped into a spire.
It pierces like an arrow of desire
That only heaven ever will remove.

Fast falls the eventide; now rings the chime
Heard by the faithful as a worship call;
But by those deaf to truth as just the fall
Of one more hour of climbing Babel's tower,
Or one more vacant night to strive to fill
With empty-minded acts of bland good will
Which time will terminate, and death devour.

Unconscious of the evening clouds that lower
While autumn sunset burns the sky with gold,
The commerce-kings rush past at Vespers hour,
As if life's meaning might be bought and sold.
Blind to the churchyard's sure and certain sign,
They miss the sun's last, horizontal ray
That shines on granite stones, foreshadowing
The lightened darkness of that final Day
For which the remnant worshippers still pray.

And do our hearts in modern times incline
To bury ancient landmarks, crumple creeds?
Yet True Jerusalem still intercedes
Amidst the clouded hills of God's design.
Thus hinges history on pew and quire,
Surviving on the embers of her fire.

Nocturnal Litany I

"From all malevolence the night employs...."
— James Agee, *Epithalamium*

From all malevolence the night employs
To haunt our ragged hearts and weary brains
With bitterness that pulses through the veins
Of memory with its unrelenting noise;
From nightmare images that hover over us
Portending toxic days, Good Lord, deliver us.

From cynicism's clamor that destroys
True faith; from dread that shadows sleep, or reigns
In dreams designed by doubt; from giving rein
To vexing fears, whose echoes hush the voice
Behind the burning bush, aflame and quiverous —
From fleeing holy ground, Good Lord, deliver us.

From vitriolic passions that disguise
Their venom as a balm while, serpentine,
They surge vindictively through every vein,
Convincing us that it will make us wise
To eat the fruit of malice that will wither us;
From all such deadly thoughts, Good Lord, deliver us.

Oh Lamb of God to whom all thoughts are bare,
All dark is light, accept our evening prayer.

Nocturnal Litany II

> "Lighten our darkness, we beseech Thee, O Lord; and by thy great mercy defend us from all perils and dangers of this night; for the love of thy only Son, our Saviour, Jesus Christ. Amen."
>
> *— The Book of Common Prayer*

From riotous rage that makes our hearts its lair
And stalks the opportunity to gain
Imagined justice for remembered pain,
Devouring health and peace and honest prayer;
From ghastly unforgiveness, that cadaverous
Attendant at hell's gate, Good Lord, deliver us.

From dabbling at the edges of despair
When daily misery seems pre-ordained,
And loss of hope that life will be explained
Starts draining our capacity to care;
When senseless circumstances turn carnivorous,
Consuming mind and flesh, Good Lord, deliver us.

When perseverance has no strength to spare,
And pessimism's thickest links of chain
Wind tightly round our hearts till we complain
That they are heavier than we can bear –
An inner suit of armor that will smother us –
Lighten our heaviness, Good Lord; deliver us.

When we would sleep with no desire to wake,
Arise, Lord God, and save us, for thy sake.

Do Not Deny the Stranger

"Life you may evade, but Death you shall not.
You shall not deny the Stranger."
        — T.S. Eliot, Choruses from *The Rock*

Give not a "Celebration of Life" when I am dead.
Give (to the small congregation my corpse might gather), instead,
The Requiem that, beneath it all,
They crave. Require them to recall
The truth, and face a full-fledged funeral.
Give the gift of this witness against denial
Along with full permission not to smile.
Shun the shallow cliches,
The fraudulent phrase.
(No, I won't survive forever in your memory or thought;
You, too, are mortal; I will not.)
So don't abandon the obvious, or pretend
That this is not a reminder of your end,
By covering facts with fake festivity
And slickly forsaking the sacred ceremony.
The memento mori is not the Enemy,
Nor is death a friend.
Refuse to avoid the vital rite that ultimately
Punctuates the inevitable universality
Of our mortality. Don't try to bury reality.
Resist the urge to bereave
Yourself of this time to grieve.
Toll the ancient bell –
It is for you, as well.

Give, to any who come, a funeral
To unearth what they know: that Death is real.
Undertake to make ceremony
Of sorrow. Allow it to terrify

You; let it unveil the adversary, verify
The vanity of vanities, disclose the disgrace
Of imagined human omnipotence. Let ritual's eloquent gravity erase
The delusion of deathlessness with its depraved pride
Which is the soul's suicide.
Let yourself be appalled that someone died.
Confront the destined danger.
Contemplate Death's reign,
If you can, till you're almost insane
With dread, distress, and anger.
Set his throne – oak, mahogany, or pine –
Where all can see its sure and certain sign.
Expose to view
Life's impotent end.
And if you at all esteem me, do
Not condescend
To gloss my life with hagiography.

This Stranger who stands in the shade at the end of the route
Has been there from the start. We've no way out.
Here, in sacred space, he wears no disguise.
Acknowledge that he will not be evaded.
This is defeat, not to be celebrated
But solemnized. Use my demise
To make known the tyrant's throne:
Read the Burial Office. Put my name and dates on a stone.

Time Heals No Ill

If Time were every mourner's salve,
As we are given to believe –
For every grief remedial,
For sorrow's ill the curative –
What pharmacy could ever fill
Enough prescriptions to relieve
The ache of all humanity's
Persistent woes? Would decades heal
Our souls' inoperable disease,
Or even many centuries
Suffice as comfort? Could they ease
Our chronic pain, or make death bearable?

When sin stole immortality
And made time subject to the Fall,
No drug could treat our malady.
Since then, life seems a terminal
Infirmity; no balm or pill
Alleviates its misery.
No length of years can make alive
The ones we grieve for, nor revive
Our earthbound spirits. What can save
Us from bereavement, and the grave,
Or free us from perpetual
Distress? Not cold, uncaring Time,
Whose ticking clock, whose ringing chime
Still tolls our endless mortal ill,
Intoning the incurable.

All Flesh is Grass

"When the ungodly are green as the grass, and when all the workers of wickedness do flourish, then shall they be destroyed forever; but thou, Lord, art the most highest for evermore."

— Psalm 92:7

"In the morning it is green, and groweth up; but in the evening it is cut down, dried up, and withered."

— Psalm 90: 6

When haughty lawless scoundrels with their boorish
Intrigues appear, like morning's grass, to neither
Be sickly nor in scarcity, but flourish
In brightest greens, while humble people wither
Like faded blades cut down and left to feed
Rogues' evil schemes – compost upon their vice –
One thinks perhaps to trade the Christian creed
For, "Some by virtue fall, and others rise
By sin." Malignant overgrowth of weeds
Appears to suffocate, with strong-willed roots,
The fairest fields and flowers, and all seeds
Except seeds of frustration, fear and doubt –
Until the evening mowers intervene,
Cut down the proud, and leave God's people green.

Curtain Call

Allow me at my end to be like these
Descending leaves that elegantly dance
Their final scene, expressing festive peace
As they take leave of life. Still colorful,
They ornament the sky as Fall's sun slants
To warm their gold, release their sweet fragrance.
They've felt their feebling stems, and known the call
Of gravity's exuberant release,
Accepting the approach of their decease
With bliss. They leave their limbs and calmly fall
In pirouettes; slow-dancing with the breeze,
They fill the air below their trees' expanse,
Content with or without an audience
To witness this performance – this, their last –
By spring's or summer's beauty unsurpassed.
Allow me, at my end, to be like these.

ACKNOWLEDGEMENTS

I would like to thank the following publications for previously publishing these poems:

First Things: "Ascension Day: Facing East", "All Flesh is Grass", and "Cutting Down Chrysanthemums"

Modern Age: "Robin on a Sculpted Stone"

The North American Anglican: "Curtain Call" and "Rondel for a Passing Year"

Measure Review: "Late Bloomers"

The Society of Classial Poets: "The Falcon", "In the Midst of Life We Are in Death", "Autumn Ecstasy", "After the Fall", and "Orchestra Tuning Up"

Most of all, I am deeply grateful to my husband/editor, Paul Erlandson, for all of his help in improving my poems, and to many friends who have encouraged my writing.

www.ingramcontent.com/pod-product-compliance
Lightning Source LLC
LaVergne TN
LVHW092327230325
806632LV00010B/457